AF620036

THE PASSAGE OF TIME

José Guilherme Correa

1st edition

Published by the author in 2012

José Guilherme Correa

THE PASSAGE OF TIME

2012

ISBN 978-1-300-01111-8

Contents:

THE PASSAGE OF TIME

P O I N T L E S S L Y
G R A D U A L L Y
C A S U A L L Y
T E D I U M
M A K E S
W A Y S
A N D
O H !
I
A M
N O T
S U R E
L O V E ' S
G O L D E N
D E S T I N Y
A P P R O V E S
A F A T E F U L
H O U R - G L A S S
LEST ANSWERS COME FROM THE DARK

LEST ANSWERS COME FROM THE DARK

While destinies are connected by the traffic
bodies are drained by avenues, streets, slopes,
viaducts, tree-lined lanes, tunnels and bridges.
Lest answers come from the dark, lights shall signal
the approaching nightfalls and the electric grids
of steel creatures, megalithic monuments
to the living, buildings often made of
plastic, glass, and wood in intense communion,
which man's mind and imagination contemplate
in acts of self-discovery and fulfilment.

Mobs are quiet, and everything is relative
while the arrow of progress points to direct,
dark nothingness as opposed to light fullness.

Light is thus a deafness-disclosing artifice.
Out of craftsmanship, light cuts shades and silhouettes.
Ah! such elusive and poor architecture!
Process is the infinite in the finite"

as Alfred North Whitehead put it so well.

Nature alone properly loves itself,"

as Wystan Hugh Auden put it so well.

Nature is the secret of the great infinite.
Nature fools us in a number of ways,
least of all the monotony of geometry.
Through briefly designed ordinary venues,
man elicited loneliness, and built.
If rocks and tress are surprisingly natural,
artificial progress does oppose nature.
Many want to part with, or fight the impulse
of moroseness by going to see places:
a short trip on amenable week ends,
revealing the wider sky or high mountain,
might as well hit ranges of dreamed surrealism:
alienations mirrored by skyscrapers,
drawing vacant spaces, reflecting waves
of solitary, mind-boggling ideas.

Loads of tobacco spurt invisibility
and sceneries imprison the palmed disquiet.
Man approaches gaiety and life spaces
just as if they sucked asphyxiate asphalt
even though Nature did not bestow Space
upon him as the finest of modalities
of escapist, recreational emptiness.

Gruesome hearts refute every flattering voice.
Disunited, angels do whisper: death.
Where's the secret? Man buried it, by building
buildings. Walls. Walls. Monotony. More buildings.
Solitude is loss of familiarity
as well as loss of the link with the infinite:
what other destination is thus driven?
The will of the Being is always definite.
Crowds generate groups and absurd communities.
God is broad. Yet no template fits solutions.
Born out of its own redolent charm, solitude,
once annulled, rests desolation and entropy.
A nontransferable cycle of loneliness
is on its way; no crowd is less than absolute,
nor many answers derived from mass customizing
which has often been seen round these dark parts.

PETRARCHAN SONNET

As I invoked the brightness of intelligence,
the cosiness of antiquated boroughs
workèd dreamlike in my mind, and arose
the heraldic point of the sun's emergence

upon my prayers for harmonic convergence.
I happened to dream of a girl named Primrose
who, having trouble to keep track of heroes,
symptomatically plotted to take vengeance

against every soul-trusting multi-facet.
I heralded the Roman goddess Flora,
and the God of Sleep whose onset I cosset.

Void of ideas, I then read the Torah,
bathed, combed and groomed my male beagle-basset
before greeting the warm, loving aurora.

INTO THE DARKNESS

1

INTO THE SEA: FROM PALOS TO GUANAHANI, 1492

The crew of the three vessels leaving Spain
looked like mourners, or maybe condemned victims
on their way to the scaffold; this despondency
was not shared by the buoyant, hope-inspired
chief commander, who for a score of years

had wandered, an idle, semi-crazed visionary,
an object of contempt for everybody.
On the main deck of the Santa Maria,
he stood, his hurts now about to be cured.
The prow pointed directly to the West.
No longer subject to the world's insults,
he was a dignified, powerful captain
at the service of European monarchs.
In the future he foresaw roseate views:
India, with its mighty Khan, shining gold-dust,
perfumes, spices, pearls, diamonds, and dyes.
He fancied the gorgeous streets of Cipango.
Proud honours would eventually be given him
in marble palaces by mighty potentates.
In his destiny he might find the domain
of Prester John, the mysterious king
whose faith, kingdom and subjects were all Christian.
Thus he dreamed and set hopes as boldly sailed
westward, plunging into unknown sea ways.
Fair weather, smooth waves and smiling skies promised
a successful and gratifying voyage.
The elements did not seem to oppose
his scope; but there were lurking dangers within,

not without the expeditionary vessels.
The very first trouble came from the failure
of Pinta's rudder; the Admiral suspected
that such damage had been arranged pre-emptively
by her own unhappy owners, the Crown.
The fleet ran into a Canary harbour,
a new rudder was arranged, and weeks later
the trip was resumed; in open sea, though,
beyond limits of the known navigation,
her occupants, losing sight of Canaries,
lost their heart as well: their known world was gone!
Sailors knew not whither the fleet was going.
They showed their grief in clamorous complaints.
Soon, the sight of a floating mast shocked them,
as an omen of the darkness beyond.
The Admiral tried to reassure them.
He disclosed visions of limitless wealth;
he appealed to their cupidity, passions,
and every other reconciling reason,
hiding, however, the number of leagues
so far navigated under false records.
In due time, trade winds and pacific waters
helped to create an atmosphere of peace.
A sea-bird of the kind that never sleeps

appeased them further: harbingers of good,
birds were as welcome as sung morning chants,
which kept the crew far from open rebellion.
The Admiral resourced to utmost patience
and watchfulness to prevent any outbreak.
The crew was happy when trade winds bore them
smoothly on; or else they feared no homecoming.
They were gratified upon meeting weeds
indicating the nearness of land, else
frightened when such weed masses were more dense;
they'd rather extricate themselves from that.
Any region where stagnant air might mean
rotting forever over windless sea
worried them, as they dreaded the calm ocean.
Placating sailors – what a stressful test!
A critical situation came up
as they convinced themselves that their commander
was but an unreliable adventurer,
imperilling their lives only to indulge
in his pointless personal purposes.
They decided therefore to fake an accident:
throw out the captain and return to Spain.
But, on the verge of being ruined by mutiny,

the expedition heard the thrilling cry
of "Land!" It was Martin Pinzon who shouted.
At once there was joy on board, but despair
replaced it overnight because such land
proved a deception; for a week, men mutineered.
Incredibly though they neither seized vessels
nor turned homeward; one night, there was some light
on the horizon; at two a.m. Pinta
roared her gun, giving the long-hoped signal.
It was the sailor Rodrigo Triana,
in the basket of the top sails, who cried,
pointed to the horizon and claimed afterwards
the reward to the first one to see land,
but the Admiral took it to himself.
His agreement with the Queen stipulated
10,000 maravedis to be bestowed
on whoever first announced the good news.
Whom should the reserved gratification
befit but the first one to see night lights?
Geophysics was about to be rewritten
on the by no means minor chess of History.

2

INTO THE UNKNOWN: MY STREAM OF PRE-AGONIC CONSCIOUSNESS

VALLADOLID, 1506

You could say that I am tall, and dignified,
of irritable, though generous temperament;
courteous of behaviour; temperate of language.
My face is oblong; my complexion, fair;
my nose, aquiline; my cheeks, protuberant.
My countenance? Definitely authoritarian!
Trouble precociously turned my hair grey.
An inflamed speaker, and a moderate dieter,
I've shown affability towards strangers,
and suavity in domestic life.

Am I the son of a humble wool-comber?
Was mine really a family of labourers?
A wildcard name I've got: I am Columbus,
Cristobal Colon, Colombo, Colonus.
I was born about 1445,
in Genoa, the eldest of four children.
However, seven other Italian cities
- Placentia, Piedmont, Savona, Oneglia,
Cogoleto, Boggiasco, and Finale -
have once claimed to be the place of my birth.

At the age of fourteen, I went to sea,
Scarcely knowing the rudiments of geography.
I did get some knowledge of navigation,
astronomy, geometry and drawing.
Between sea travels, whenever ashore,
I used to work as a book and map peddler.
So, at a most immature of stages
I was at one time a student, a sailor
and a working teenager; in due time,
I'd go from poor tramp to wealthy viceroy,
from bare-footed vagrant to welcome guest
and bosom friend of European sovereigns.
From despise to a flood of adulation,
from ambitious heroism to decay,
from glorious fame to rusty chains of iron,
in short, from cradle to ultimate bed
I have been a man of uncertain qualities,
about whom not very much is spread out.
In 1470, I settled down
in Savona, where I opened a tavern.
Fortune, however, betrayed me as publican,
so I joined a Portuguese expedition
exploring the eastern African coasts.
Their maritime operations were legendary.

Meanwhile we landed at Madeira Island,
I married the daughter of the late governor
Perestrello, who gave birth to my Diego.
I already firmly believed the theory
of the earth's globular form; sailing westward,
one would certainly reach the shores of India.
Strangers from all parts resorted to Lisbon
to participate in those enterprises,
from learned scholars to curious adventurers.
I was a face in such a crowd of thousands.
In Iceland, in 1477,
I had had the chance of familiarizing
with the sagas and voyages of Vikings.
I was also convinced that Corte Real,
a Portuguese, and John Szkolny, a Pollack,
had managed to sail westward and land somewheres.
In Portugal, the legendary Prince Henry
(unfortunately he no longer lived)
had designed milestone hydrographic charts,
which captured the attention of the world.
Well, King John II granted me audience.
My proposal consisted in securing
a shorter route to Africa by striking

directly westward across the Atlantic.
The sovereign, though reluctant to indulge
in providing the necessary ships, men
and huge expenses, finally referred
the auspicious matter to a special junta
composed of cosmographers and a bishop,
who had been responsible for perfecting
the astronomers' tables and the astrolabe,
allowing to know the height of the sun,
the angle it formed above the horizon,
and the actual distance from the equator.
Vessels, thanks to the compass and the astrolabe
could henceforth venture into unknown waters,
no longer sailing parallel to land.
I gave the junta a plan of the voyage,
with all the documents in my possession,
but they treated my project as extravagant,
and, on the pretence of bearing provisions,
dispatched a caravel with instructions
to secretly follow my ascribed route.
While I waited, having had been asked for time,
a ship did check out the pointed direction
in order to test my theory's bases:
The vessel sailed west for several days

and saw but an immeasurable ocean
and stormy weather; my project was ridiculed.
I declined further business after learning
of such nerve, and such a blatant attempt.
I bore no grudges, though, against the Portuguese.
Somehow they ill treated me, nonetheless
the main cause of my precipitate exit
were my debts, proof of which is the fine letter
that King John II addressed to me:
"And why perchance would you have any fear
for our justice by virtue of anything
to which you are obliged, we through this letter
assure you for the coming and returning,
that you shall not be arrested, retained,
accused, cited or demanded for anything,
and by the same letter we send our justices
that it should be thus." Thus spoke Rei Dom João.
Whilst I went to Italy, I dispatched
my brother Bartholomew to Great Britain
to lay my scheme before Henry VII.
He brought no positive results, though, and
I thought of offering my services to Spain.
King Ferdinand of Aragon was loathsome

and duplicitous, treating me with scepticism,
but his wife, Queen Isabella of Castile
and Leon held the opposite behaviour
What was much helpful for me was the fact
that I'd been noted for my strict religiousness,
for my regular observation of
the Catholic church's liturgical ceremonies.
Allowing for a touch of superstition,
Nothing was more remarkable on me
than my piety and charity; yet
my ambition was eager, and ungovernable;
my bigotry sometimes displaced my gentleness.
There would be no priest in my expedition.
I did not disobey the Inquisition.
I was somewhat fanatically intolerant
in the conversion of the irreligious.

I'm bald, I'm nearly blind, I've just returned
from the Indies for the fourth and last time.
I am now living with two of my sons
and seven servants, in one of the houses
where the Kingdom lodges her eminent figures.
The maid's just rubbed my forehead with a towel.
A serial vertigo of live images

and phantasmagoria cross my mind.
My soul is defeated by profound melancholy.
My body suffers from physical weakness
as well as from cruel moral dejection.
As a deep silence overtakes the house,
Franciscan friars trace crosses and read,
in a mumbling tone, the Book of the Dead.
The Reign is gloomy; her future, uncertain.
May, the slowest of months, mourns the Queen's death.
My first-born son has just married the future
Duchess of the great Ducal House of Alba,
heiress Doña Maria de Toledo.
The recently widowed King and his Minister,
Cardinal Cisneros are less preoccupied
with granting my claims, which they deem untimely,
than curing the serious ills corroding
the social cement of Spain by and large.
Castile sounds like egotism, or ungratefulness.
I still suffer with the infinite patience
accompanying me like my very shadow.
Yet I trust that royal justice shall recognize
one day the greatness of my rendered services,
and restore my privileges, at least

– that's for me an absolute point of honour –
for my heirs – that's the treasury's commitment.
I cannot deny that I am acquainted
with the throne's burden caused by constant errors,
both political and administrative.
Embittering royal procrastination!
It makes me desperate, object of dishonour,
hatred, calumny, and a world of evils.
Castillian justice's but a slender thread!

I used to be allured by fables and
exaggerations about Marco Polo,
Cipango, Prester John, the Khan of Tartary,
creations of Munchausens, and romancers,
childhood fantasies with resplendent mandarins.
I've lived a Viceroy's agitated life,
along years of audacious ocean voyaging,
full of incredulous, devious courtesans,
juntas, commissions, derisions, and mockeries,
riots, enmity, contempt and lost titles,
not to mention shipyard shuttles and lathes.
Evasive hypocrisy caused my heartbreak.
I remember the pirates and revolts,
the chieftains and the parrots of the Indies,

the gold and the silver claimed by the Spanish,
the Te Deum tolled by Catalan bells
announcing my return with jubilation.
I've lived the twilight of chivalry principles,
the decline of the spirit of the crusades,
the new European era of capitalism.
the cherished face of Philippa Moniz
and the love of Beatriz in Gomera
counterbalanced my managerial flaws,
my inability to control men,
and the shortcomings of multiple conquests.
La Navidad, or instance, was an Eden
when I found it, sudden hell when I ruled it.
Pinzon ran off with a part of the fleet.
The colonies conspicuously decayed.
My men started to die like rotten sheep.
Once imprisoned, all my assets were seized;
my depression, heightened by my anxiety;
my constitution, weakened by the illnesses
my life flame, at long last ruined and aborted.
The simple gentle folk of Valladolid
has always looked at me with curiosity.
There's only the future to enlighten

the memory of feats hardly believable.

The approaching end had me make preparations
to leave businesses in shape for successors.
My first will was a military codicil,
because testamentary dispositions
of this kind are executed by soldiers
at their point of death, without the formalities
required by the Spanish civil law.
Now, I'm executing a final codicil,
bequeathing my estates with better judgement
My son Diego is heir to my titles,
honours, prerogatives and tenths; my bastard
son, Fernandico has also been cared for.
Bartholomew Fieschi, my third son, ditto.
All my successors should serve Christian kings.
Poor relatives and people in necessity
are hereby granted liberal allowances.
A chapel shall be built in Hispaniola,
where daily masses shall honour my soul
as well as those of my mother, and wife.
Small sums are to be paid at different points ,
though where they'll came from I won't specify.
To keep the size and worth of these bequests

made by means of a testamentary codicil
written on a blank page of a prayer book
which Pope Alexander VI gave me,
all heirs are expected to do their best.
I leave this book to the Genoese public
and make Genoa the successor of
my privileges and dignities, in case
my mate line runs out. As regards Beatriz ,
thus I've candidly spoken to Diego:
□gPlease do so for the discharge of my conscience,
which weighs so heavily upon my soul!”
I've received in devotion the last sacrament.
God has always helped me through pain and glory.
My mission, if any, has been fulfilled.
Everything signed, I summon to my headboard
my legitimate son, and advise him
of his mainstream behaviour to observe:
he shall conduct the domestic accounts
so as to prevent ruin by all means!
Local bells toll the Ascension – it's Sunday,
May 20th - I hear God's call; I cry;
my lips murmur Christ's words: “In manus tuas,
Domine, commendo spiritum meum.”

3

EPILOGUE

As sorrowful tears spilled onto the faces
of Fernandico and Bartolomeo Fieschi,
Don Diego Colón Moniz, the new Admiral
(Almirante de La Mar Oceana)
promptly ordered the funeral provisions
to be carried out in the parish of
Santa María de la Antígua.
His father had shown contradictory qualities,
but he was definitely deprived of vices
typical of his contemporary Spaniards,
such as greed and disregard for the properties,
rights and lives of the new continent's natives,
to whom he gave mainly love and respect
rather than burned huts, gashed bodies, and ruins,
everything that the fierce Conquistadors
substituted for peace, and implemented.
Oddly pertinacious in his rank rescuing,
he'd miserably failed to provide Castile
with the promised and coveted spices,
groceries, precious stones and metals; instead,
he'd sent them ships loaded with slaves to sell;
he had used such money to compensate

for the expenses of four troublesome journeys.
He did believe he found a shorter route
and, therefore, a different approach to India,
hence the name "West Indies" given to hundreds
of new westward islands, which he discovered.
He sailed after absurd impossibilities,
by no means having in view a new world.
His project was not the scheme of a geographer,
but that of an ambitious navigator,
anxious to become rich by opening up
a permanent and lucrative position.
As a colonial, self-conceited governor,
he witnessed Cubans being mutilated;
during the years he governed the island,
Cacique Cahonaboa was treacherously
lured with gifts, then arrested, in Cibao.
One third of Hispaniola's population
ended most brutally exterminated.
Unable to prevent bloodsheds, he backed
conversion means including death and slavery.
To the end, he believed he had reached Asia.
He never heard at all the name America.

Not even his bones were allowed to rest.
There's no certainty as to where they're buried.
From Valladolid they went to Seville,
then to Haiti, and Cuba; it's not sure
that the remains exhumed at San Domingo
were his; the question is an open one.
After many centuries, graves and doubts
Genoa erected a stately statue,
yet the city failed to claim his ashes.
Shall history see in his stamina
an answer to the Portuguese rejection
and the indifference of the English King?
Neither conquered the honour of discovering
the very bravest of New Worlds, outsourcing
third hands, which pulled the chestnuts from the fire!
Let's only speculate, had John and Henry
favourably held Columbus' applications:
we would probably have been spared the bigotry,
horrors, butchery, atrocities, robberies,
cruelties, which the Inquisition triggered.
However chivalrous, Castile submitted him
to court judgement and two months in a dungeon.
Similar treatments befit common bandits,
but which common bandits commend their spirits

by murmuring “Onto Thy hands, O Domine,
spiritum meum commendo”? Not many.

MALLARMÉ'S “LE VIERGE, LE VIVACE ET LE BEL AUJOURD'HUI”

The virgin, the lively and the gorgeous today
Are about to tear us with a drunk blow of wings
This hard, forgotten lake haunted under the frost
By the transparent glacier of non-fleeing flights!
A swan of yesteryear remembers its magnificent,

Though hopeless, self-deliverance that did not sing
The area where life upon the sterile winter
Was surrounded by the cold of resplendent tedium.
The bird's entire neck is shaking such white agony
Throughout space inflicted upon the denying swan,
But not the horror of the soil where plumage's taken.
A phantom thereto assigning is purest glare,
It's immobilized by the cold dream of contempt,
Which the Swan wears in its futile, useless exiles.

OCTAVIO PAZ'S “TESTIMONIOS”

The ruins of the light and of the shapes worship,
Love, your dense shadow , the shadow to which
my panting breath rushes, a living tree
in lightnings grown, before its confused rumour

A god, Love, frenzied and obscure, a god
alive, without a name and without speech,
moves by the tenebrous silence in cantos
my undone tongue in a scream, the slow universe
into a flame, which in its fiery breast
hides another fire, insatiable, secret,
and fearful; by this flame nightingales moan,
children, shapes, whirlwinds of semen, tears , cries
cross the night until their exasperated
flood of foam breaks down the earth's boundaries.

Through this living flame dies the world, raised into
amorous splendours, and the women run
through the earth, mad horses on thirsty watercourses,
alike black streams of heartbeats, till they cover,
in their terrible breath, the motionless
star of my flesh; by this tibial flame
blood is flowing , in my ears storm is bursting,
my charred tongue is becoming mute, we run

along a bridge of heartbeats till we reach
death and emptiness; by this occult flame
I, the witness, put out the world, and raze
everything alive without loving it.

I recognize its shape among the shadows,
and I sink down into its blood, forever.

SOR JUANA INÉS DE LA CRUZ'S SONNET "A LA ESPERANZA"

Green spellbinder of human life,
Ah! Insane Hope, golden Frenzy,
dream of men awake, intricate
as in dreams, of treasures vainglorious;

the world's Soul, flourishing senility,
decrepit imagined Verdure,
the Today the lucky expect,
and the Morrow of the unlucky.

Let your name be followed by those

who search for your day, seeing all,
through their green spectacles, painted
as they like it. Lucky wise me:

I keep in my hands both my eyes
and only what I touch I see!

RUBÉN DARÍO'S "YO PERSIGO UNA FORMA"

I seek a form that does not meet my shape,
buds of thought that aim at a rose, or guess
that the promised kiss on my lip is less
than a Milo Venus' nonsense embrace.

Green palms bedecked the white colonnade;
stars foretold me the vision of the Goddess;
on my soul rested light, just like the restless
bird of the moon above a placid lake.
And I find but the word that does not grow,
the melody start that from the flute flows,
and the ferryboat of dreams in space sailing

and beneath my fair Sleeping Beauty's window
just the constant sigh of the fountain's flow,
and the neck of the great white swan that's questioning
me

SÁ DE MIRANDA'S SONNET "ESTE RETRATO VOSSO É O SINAL"

This picture of yours is the sign long-sighted,
far from what you are, for these eyes derelict
let me know thereby that nothing so lit
might properly by mortal eyes be sighted.

What eyes have ever naturally pictured,
or seen the sun, or a far-away lighthouse,
even if clouds make less, in a dark night,
of an obstacle? Same with your eyes mixture.
For were such unexpected eyes from face
to face by the painter to a cure likened
and gotten rightly as he saw you smiling,
I still would not know what he might have traced,

as Grace in your smile is never weakened.

Not to say speaking? Not to say laughing?

JACQUES PRÉVERT (from 'Fatras')

As life finishes playing
Death puts everything in place
Life is fun
Death cleans the household
Regardless of the dust he hides under the carpet
So many good things he forgets
(e.g. the beautiful life)

RUMI's random touchstones

(i) Let the beauty lovèd be what you do.

(ii) As love unites everything, all is well.

(iii) You were born with wings. Why crawl throughout life?

(iv) Your way of love is God's will toward you.

(v) Only from the heart can you can touch the sky.

(vi) The beauty of the heart is the lasting beauty.

(vii) Through love I became the giver of light.

(viii) The touch of the spirit on the body / 's one kiss we long for through life. Love's life's water.

MARCOS KONDER REIS' "Acende no meu peito o sério lume"

Light in my bosom the serious fire

Lit in your dirty, benighted breast,

And be in my fear, in my torment,

The favourite master, beloved god

Apt to light, under the shoal of stars,

A road which fills my country of love,

Detained from everything that turned you,

in the world, into composted manure.

PIERRE RÉVERDY's 'HORIZON' (fragment)

The dream, as heavy as ham, hangs from the ceiling

as the ash of your cigar contains the whole light.

Around the corner trees suffer, the sun assassin bleeds

the pines and those who cross the wet meadow.

The evening when the first owl fell asleep I was drunk.

My soft limbs hang here and the sky supports me,

the sky where I wash my eyes every morning.

My red hand is a word,

a brief appeal where a sob throbs blood

poured onto the filter paper.
Ink costs nothing.

I walk on spots that are ponds among black streams

going beyond the end of the world where I'm expected.

This is either the fountain or the blood drops

flowing from my heart, which one hears.

A bugle in the azure sounds the call.

GEORGES SEFERIS' 'Love Song'

You searched, destiny rose, how to hurt,

But stooped like a secret ready to abort

Nice was the order you agreed to institute

Your smile like a sword held high in the air.

It warned nature of your rising nest

From your thorn departed the half-dreamed road

Naked and keen to possess you, we dawned

The world was simple, but a pounding heart.

SOUSANDRADE's "Dos rubros flancos do redondo oceano" (from the cycle 'Golden Harps')

By the crimson flanks of the round ocean

With its wings of light holding the land

I saw the sun rising, young and beautiful

Scrambling by way of its golden shoulders

A fragrant bright coma on the face

Of a fire lighted by love which

A smile of coral left wandering by.

Around me bring not thy rays, sun fire!

Stand up and proceed, hear not my harp

Ye whom once in candid songs I greeted.

SOUSANDRADE's 'O Guesa Errante' (fragment)

Large grape-stomping vats under the light shine.

Oh! how beautiful this summer day is!
A sea dragon, waves roared onto its wings
Likewise, on its bulk an untamed volcano!
Moodily reclined over the deck, Guesa,
The wandering one, walked on by to and fro,
Mute, restless, fast, fickle, in disarray
Both his mantle and forehead never whiter
His hair in disorder, his face as pale
As his dreams' nightly beat...
"Wake up, my eyes!" [...]

PAOLO TOSTI's Amaranth Song

Nina's marriage proposal and winning home run
rival my serenading!
Ah, dear flower of amaranth! Marry, yet I won't budge!
Amid celebratory smiles & flowers,
no thoughts for our love of old?
Day and night, my song'll groan for you, full of passion.
Ah, my mint leaf and garnet flower!

Forget not the kisses I gave you!

MATHILDE WESENDONCK's five Lieder

(i) From 'The angel':

In early childhood I often heard of angels' (sublime joy of heaven)

Replacing the soil with sun

so that, when a heart bang in worries

it languishes hidden from the world

(ii) From 'Stand still!':

Blessed in sweet oblivion,

I appreciate all possible delights!

When in August, the eye's blissful drinking

Sinks into the soul; and nature is found again,

Hopefully everything is announcing the end;
The silent lip, in silence marveling,

No longer wants to bear witness to the requested inner being.

(iii) From 'In the greenhouse':

High arched crown leaves,

Canopies of Smaragad, children from remote areas,

Tell me, why do you complain? ...

Well, I know, poor plant:

A fate we share,

Whether illuminated by light and splendour,

Our homeland is not here!

And how gladly the sun separates

From the day an empty sham, ...

Heavy drops I see hovering

At the leaves' green hem.

(iv) From 'Pain':

The Sun weeps every night like your beautiful red eyes

When, bathing in the sea, an early death reaches you;

buy your former glory, though, glory of the gloomy world,
and re-awake in the morning, as a proud victory hero!

Delights only give pain;

Oh how I thank that

Such natural pain be given me!

(v) From 'Dreams':

Tell me, what wonderful dreams, keeping my mind embraced,

do not, like empty foams, have passed into bleak nothingness?

Dreams that, every hour, every day more beautifully bloom,

and, with their blessed astronomy,

draw through the mind!

Dreams, like the lofty beams, sink into the soul,

there, forever, to paint a picture,

to, dreaming, donate their fragrance, gently burn up to

your chest, and then sink into the grave.

RAFAEL ALBERTI's sonnet 'To Federico García Lorca'

Go out, drink villages seaward
turn yourself a water deer
and bend toward the white clarities
of the kingfisher's rocked nest;

I'll go, deadened, wait for you,
turnèd reed, on the high solitudes,
wounded by air and required
by your lone voice among storms.

Let me write, o weak reed cold,
my name on these running waters,
which the wind, lonely, calls river.

My name dissolved on your snow,
go back to your climbing mountains,
deer of foam, king of the river-hill."

VICENTE ALEIXANDRE's Sonnet

What firm architecture, so keen
on beauty, so orderly, rises
from landscape, and enters the certainty
of the air (no wrath) to supplant it?

The bass lines do. But from its plant
the curve springs, upholds its correctness
at the top, and respects the bark
intact, a prison for much pomp.

The high sky thoughtful lights divides
into rhythms of imponent cults,
that cheifly achieve their straight mandate.

Its nuances (no iris) the dwellings
of the air yield, vibrating, hidden,
and the total chord claims perfection.

VALERY'S CIMETIERE MARIN

This quiet roof, where doves wander about,
Throbs among the pines, among the sepulchres;
Fair southern noon thereupon compounds flames
The sea, the sea, always recommencing
Oh reward in the aftermath of thought,
Longly regarding the calm of the gods!

What pure work of fine flashes consumes many
Diamonds made of imperceivable foam!
And what a peace seems to be conceived!
When above the abyss a sun is resting,
Purest working of an eternal cause,
The time scintillates, and the dream is knowledge

Stable treasure, simple Minerva temple,
A mass of calm, and visible reserve,
Supercilious water, thy guarding Eye
Of so much sleep under a veil of flame,
O my silence! . . . Building within the soul,
Golden ceiling with a thousand tiles. Roof!

Temple of Time, which a unique sigh summarizes,
At this pure point I climb and get accustomed,
Alone, surrounded by my marine glance;
And, as my supreme offering to the gods,
Over altitude a sovereign disdain
Is sowed by the waves' serene scintillation.

As the fruit is merged into enjoyment,
It changes its absence in like deliciousness
Inside a mouth where its shape dies itself,
I hereupon inhale my future smoke
And the heavens sing to the consumed soul
The transformation of banks into rumour.

Beautiful sky, true sky, see how I change!
After so much pride, after so much strange
Idleness, nevertheless full of power,
To this brilliant space I abandon myself;
My shadow, whose frail drive imprisons me,
Crosses the resting places of the dead,

O my soul exposed to the solstice's torches,
I do sustain you, admirable justice
Of light whose weapons are without pity!
I tighten you purely, at your prime place.
Look at yourself! . . . To provide light, however,
Presumes a dull half of shadow.

Oh for myself, in myself, to myself,
Near a heart, at the sources of the poem,
Between the void and the pure event,
I wait the echo of my inner grandeur,
Most bitter, sombre and sonorous reservoir,
Sounding forever the soul's hollow future!

Know you, false captive of the foliages, gulf
Eater of meagre nettings, dazzling secrets
Despite my closed eyes, know what body drags
Me to its lazy end? Know you what face
Attracts such body to this bone-full ground?
A spark thinks there in my absent loved ones.

Closed, sacred, plenty of fire without matter,
Earthly fragments offered to heaven's light,
These plots, dominated by torches, please me,
Composed by gold, by stone and by dark trees;
Where much marble trembles over much shadows;
The faithful sea there sleeps over my tombs!

Draw the idolater aside, splendid bitch!
Whenever alone with a shepherd's smile,
I pasture for quite long (mysterious sheep)
The white flock of my tranquil sepulchres;
The prudent doves, vain dreams, and curious angels:
Now drive them far away away away!

The newly-arrived future is idleness.
The net insect scrapes the barrenness;
All is burned, undone, drawn up in the air
To I know not which severe essence...
Life is vast, and it is drunk with absence;
Bitterness is sweet, and spirit is clair.

The hidden dead are all right in this earth
Which warms them by drying away their mystery.
Midday up there, southern noon without movement
On itself brooding, to itself appropriate,
The head complete and the diadem perfect,
I am within you the secret changing.

You only have me to refrain your fears!
My repentances, my doubts, my constraints
Make up the flaws in your grand diamond!...
But in their heavy, marble-cumbered night,
A vague people under the roots of trees
Has already sided with you, slowly.

They have melted into a thick absence,
For the red clay has drunk the white species;
The gift of life has passed into the flowers!
Where are, of the dead, the familiar phrases,
Personal artistry and singular souls?

The larvae have slipped by where cries were formed.

The sharp screams of the teased girls, the eyes,
The teeth, the wet eyelids, the charming bosom
That plays with fire, the blood that shines when
The lips are yielded and surrendering,
The last gifts, the fingers that defend them,
Everything goes to earth, and joins the game!

And you, great soul, do you expect a dream
No longer with such hues of lies which toward
Fleshly eyes the wave and the gold make here?
Will you still sing when you are vaporous?
Go! everything flees! my presence is porous;
And saintly impatience does also die!

Meagre immortality, black and golden,
Frighteningly laurelled consoler, which
Out of death makes a maternal bosom,
A beautiful lie, and a pious trick!
Who does not know, and who refuses them -
- That empty skull and that eternal laugh?!

Deep down fathers, uninhabited heads,
Which, under the weight of so many pellets,
Are indeed the earth, and confound our steps,
The real rodent, the worm irrefutable
Is not for you who sleep under the table,
He's fed by life itself, he doesn't leave me!

Is it love, maybe, or hatred of myself?
His secret tooth is so close to me that
Any name absolutely suits him well!
Mind you, he sees, wants, dreams, touches my flesh,
Which pleases him even upon my layers!

I live to pertain to this living being!

Zeno, Zeno, cruel philosopher Zeno,
Have you then pierced me with your feathered arrow
That hums and flies, yet does not fly! The sounding
Shaft gives me life, the arrow kills. Oh, sun! --
Oh, what a tortoise-shadow to outrun
My soul, Achilles' giant stride left standing!

Zeno! Cruel Zeno! Zeno of Elea!
Have you pierced me with that winged arrow
That vibrates, flies and does not fly! the sound
Gives birth to me, and the arrow kills me!
Oh! the sun, the sun... what a turtle-shadow
For the soul, Achilles' large steps inertial!

No, no!... Upright! In the successive era!
Break, my body, this meditative form!
And drink, my breast, to the birth of the wind!
A freshness, exhalation from the sea,
Restores my soul... O salted potency!
Let us run to the wave in live flash backs.

Yes! Yes! great delirious sea, endowed with
Panther skin and perforated chlamydia,
By the sun's thousand and thousand idols,
Absolute hydra, drunk on your blue flesh,
That re-bites at your most glittering tail
In a tumult with similar silence
The wind rises!... trying to live is mandatory!
The immense air opens and shuts my book,
The dusty wave dares spout out from the rocks!
Do fly away, my much dazzled pages!
Break, waves! break, from the delighted waters,

This quiet roof where seals were pecking.

DÉCIO PIGNATARI'S "POEMA"

Coarse sayings about fluid things,
Razor-sharped edges tearing the wind:
So many weeks existing
And living – of one moment a single hint.
Scrambled prism of the nymph's
Retina which puts to sleep worlds with no clout
Plummet, the light that wounds it loses its route,
Clears the submarine lymph:
Buildings dive branches of cement,
Of eyes into pebble clots neons become the givers,
And corners wound the flanks of those fish-less rivers
Of which I am the source, and a shipwreck victim upon the intent

ANTONIO MACHADO'S "HÚMEDO ESTÁ BAJO EL LAUREL EL BANCO"

Damp, under the laurel,

is the green-stone bench;
the rain has washed off
from the white wall's top
the ivy leaves' dust.
The fall wind's warm breath
ripples the lawns whilst
the poplar grove talks
to the evening wind
in the shrubbery!
Meanwhile, the twilight,
refreshed by the grape-brunches
on the vine, is bright,
and the good bourgeois,
on his balcony,
lights his stoical pipe
where smokes his tobacco,
I go on remembering
my juvenile verses...
What's become of that
sonorous heart mine?
Is it true that you'll
depart, gentle shadows,
flying off among
the goldenest trees?

HUIDOBRO'S "NIPONA"

Arise,
Rare flowers

From the paradise
(that Yoshiwara of ours).
And you, my little Japanese doll,
Come together – let our yearning roam,
Having the marvellous turquoise pool roll
Under the sky that extends its onyx canopy's foam.
Let my kisses
Touch your slanting
Face - it misses
An evil panting,
A brutal desire.
Let'em so, t'is
Thus I admire
You: as a biscuit
Our eyes are two oval-shaped and enervating drops
Your face yellow and made of ivory seems
And your piercing charm tops
All fictitious, rare dreams.
See, white and odorous
On the veneer,
The roses'
Tear.

www.ingramcontent.com/pod-product-compliance
Ingram Content Group UK Ltd.
Pitfield, Milton Keynes, MK11 3LW, UK
UKHW020231250726
13967UKWH00001B/308